© **Look forward in your life**
BY SANDEEP RAVIDUTT SHARMA

Table of Contents

Foreword IV
Look forward in your life............................1

© **Look forward in your life**
BY SANDEEP RAVIDUTT SHARMA

Foreword

This book provides you with a list of 100 quotes and thoughts about LIFE, churned out by my mind with the consciousness, grace and energy of **Shiva Shakti**. I'm sure if you keep reading, referring, sharing these thoughts and quotes about **LIFE**, you may derive inspiration and develop good understanding of various perspectives and facts. Happiness and sorrow keep influencing your life. Don't let your past influence your future, focus on today and you can create a beautiful tomorrow.

"Look forward in your life and regrets are no more. Keep going with each step forward. Happiness awaits you at every step."

I sincerely hope, you will find this book amazing, interesting, rejuvenating, unique and a constant source of Inspiration.

Thank You and Happy Reading.

© Look forward in your life
BY SANDEEP RAVIDUTT SHARMA

© Copyright 2018 Sandeep Ravidutt Sharma - All rights reserved.

In no way is it legal to reproduce, duplicate, or transmit any part of this document in either electronic means or in printed format. Recording of this publication is strictly prohibited and any storage of this document is not allowed unless with written permission from the publisher. All rights reserved. The information provided herein is stated to be truthful and consistent, in that any liability, in terms of inattention or otherwise, by any usage or abuse of any policies, processes, or directions contained within is the solitary and utter responsibility of the recipient reader. Under no circumstances will any legal responsibility or blame be held against the author / publisher for any reparation, damages, or monetary loss due to the information herein, either directly or indirectly. The author own all copyrights.

Legal Notice:
This book is copyright protected. This is only for personal use. You cannot amend, distribute, sell, use, quote or paraphrase any part or the content within this book without the consent of the author or copyright owner. Legal action will be pursued if this is breached.

Disclaimer Notice:
Please note the information contained within this book is for motivational, educational and knowledge sharing purpose only. Every attempt has been made to provide the reader accurate, up to date and reliable complete information. No warranties of any kind are expressed or implied. Readers acknowledge that the author is not engaging in the rendering of legal, financial, medical or professional advice. By reading this document, the reader agrees that under no circumstances the author / publisher is responsible for any losses, direct or indirect, which are incurred as a result of the use of information contained within this document, including, but not limited to errors, omissions, or inaccuracies.

If you have further questions, contact on **Tel: +919969256731**
Email: sandeepraviduttsharma@gmail.com

© **Look forward in your life**
BY SANDEEP RAVIDUTT SHARMA

Dedication

This book is dedicated to **Shiva Shakti** - the epitome of love. **Lord Shiva** is pure consciousness symbolising the masculine principle. **Goddess Shakti** symbolises the active feminine energy of **Shiva** and is synonymously identified with **Tripura Sundari, Sati** or **Parvati**.

These primal principles are also called as **PURUSHA** representing consciousness and **PRAKRITI** denoting the nature. Shiva and Shakti are manifestations of the all-in-one divine consciousness. Shiva is the paternal love of God that gives us consciousness, knowledge and clarity. Shakti is the motherly love of God that showers warmth, care and ensures our protection. Shiva and Shakti exist within each of us as the masculine and feminine energy.

To please **Shiva Shakti** praying for the well being, love, happiness, strength, positive energy and success of my readers in their life, I hereby recite the following mantra...

"Sarva Mangala Mangalye Shive Sarvartha Sadhike Sharanye Tryambake Gauri Narayani Namostute"

© **Look forward in your life**
BY SANDEEP RAVIDUTT SHARMA

Photo Credits

The beautiful and amazing photograph used for the book cover is clicked by **Nilgün Kanık** from **Turkey.**

You can visit her excellent photo gallery at **Instagram: @nlgncan**

Look forward in your life

© **Look forward in your life**
BY SANDEEP RAVIDUTT SHARMA

Ideas prefer to accompany those who are ready to execute.

© **Look forward in your life**
BY SANDEEP RAVIDUTT SHARMA

Come out of your comfort zone by accepting newer challenges.

If your soul controls your mind and body, you can do no wrong.

Relax only when you have reached your destination in time.

Remember to get down at your destination else you will miss out all those who are waiting to cheer for you.

Not everyone acts when opportunity knocks. Those who do, know it to be the opportunity.

© **Look forward in your life**
BY SANDEEP RAVIDUTT SHARMA

Don't wear the mask of ignorance when people expect you to know everything and lead them to victory.

© **Look forward in your life**
BY SANDEEP RAVIDUTT SHARMA

Prayer connects you to the Lord directly without the need of a mediator or a translator.

Real freedom is felt when you ignore order of others directing you to change your life.

Understanding follows listening and precedes resolution.

© **Look forward in your life**
BY SANDEEP RAVIDUTT SHARMA

Losing temper is easy against someone's anger. Try to maintain your cool at all times.

If your roots are strong. You can branch out and reach to the whole world.

When you surrender to the almighty God. Fear dies down and no more dictates your action.

Nature is magnificent and makes us realise how small we really are. The most powerful and the richest person on earth are not equivalent to a grain against the vastness of nature. Mother Nature has got no eGo and cares for all.

© Look forward in your life
BY SANDEEP RAVIDUTT SHARMA

Roll up your sleeves and pick up the axe not to cut down the live trees but to cut down the dead wooden logs into pieces which can make your furniture.

© **Look forward in your life**
BY SANDEEP RAVIDUTT SHARMA

Fantastic day always begins with you.

Don't insist on others to declare you as a winner instead earn it through a scintillating performance.

The relationship of decades is lost in a second due to ego. Shed your ego and develop good understanding.

*Don't gamble with your time.
Time never looks back.*

Answer in time when your roll call is announced.

Take up the laughter challenge and you don't get affected by failure anymore.

© **Look forward in your life**
BY SANDEEP RAVIDUTT SHARMA

Touching the summit makes you feel on top of the world.

© **Look forward in your life**
BY SANDEEP RAVIDUTT SHARMA

The creator has given the same gift of dreams to both achievers and losers. It's the efforts which separate them.

© **Look forward in your life**
BY SANDEEP RAVIDUTT SHARMA

Don't wait in the dark. No one would notice your existence. Make attempt to at least touch the light on your own. Many hands which are kind enough are waiting to lift and save you.

Don't wait for Angels to come and rescue, instead become one.

© **Look forward in your life**
BY SANDEEP RAVIDUTT SHARMA

Everyone wants to run faster and climb the ladder of success in no time. In the process of reaching greater heights if you have not lived your life then such success would be meaningless.

Joyfulness attract people around you.

Facing challenges becomes easy when you treat them as opportunities.

Alter your thought pattern towards positivity by making your mind remember that you are here with a purpose which is clean, kind and full of love.

Winners don't shy away from taking responsibility.

Flowers bloom and showers happiness all around

© **Look forward in your life**
BY SANDEEP RAVIDUTT SHARMA

Those who aim for the Sky looking to meet the Stars would never dive into the Sea for pearls.

Take advice but that doesn't mean stop thinking on your own.

Avoid speaking harsh words, instead practice silence for sometime.

Winning starts and ends with you.

Pray, and your wishes will be answered.

Those who are compassionate can understand others pain and hardship.

Everyone wants to grow rich but not all put in the required efforts.

With passage of time one realises the true meaning and value of wait and patience.

Shed yesterday's baggage of glory or humiliation. Today is another day.

When someone presents you a gift, accept it happily with lots of appreciation, gratitude, and positivity would multiply.

Those who are mentally stressed don't know what they are talking or have talked about. Unload all your thoughts and take a break from the routine.

Winning or losing is not in your hands but more or less it's in your mind.

Keep Smiling, and you can win the world.

Don't wait or take a break when it's time for you to perform.

Instead of passing judgement about others, try to understand their view.

Prayer for the day: It's a great day to start with. Everyone and everything are favourable. I'm here to win.

Alone you stand in the Ocean of sorrow. Hundreds would surround you in moments of joy. Be the same person whether you experience sorrow or happiness.

The dark impression on a colourful environment is still better than on a black background as it may get lost in the process.

Illusion has many faces. It becomes reality if you believe.

Not every winner knows how to celebrate. winning attitude and die hard performance can make your day.

© **Look forward in your life**
BY SANDEEP RAVIDUTT SHARMA

Don't quit when someone tells or yells. You are here to win and not to permanently carry losers tag.

Motivating self or others is a recurring activity.

When opportunities knocks, you have to open the door in a welcome and thankful mode. Opportunities doesn't like frowning faces.

Look into the future only when you have fulfilled today's responsibility.

Relaxed mind helps one to take a nap anywhere while sleep eludes one with disturbed mind even in the most luxurious bed.

Each one of us is unique creation of the Lord and still looks similar. Uniqueness come to the fore only when the glow of knowledge, sincerity and determined efforts merge with your personality.

Prepare yourself for any kind of eventuality when you have decided to face challenges head-on.

Keep turning the pages of your life and be ready for the surprises.

Let the hope of life bloom like a flower and spread the fragrance of love all around.

Darkness can only laugh till the first ray of the sun appears.

© **Look forward in your life**
BY SANDEEP RAVIDUTT SHARMA

Never get influenced by others unless they inspire and bring positivity in your life.

Relationship blossoms when selfishness is no more.

Sometimes you spend your entire life time to find the purpose of your life.

Attempt to understand others and avoid conflicts.

Never wait for results if you have executed your task well. You know the result already.

Mirror hides nothing. It can clearly tell your state of mind. When you can't hide your emotions before the man made object - a mirror. Forget about hiding it from the almighty God. The Creator knows it all. Pray with purity of thoughts, and it will be answered soon.

It is not important as to how much knowledge do you have and what you can do. It is more important to see what you can do now.

Take a look at your own self at least once in a day. Greet your own self into the mirror with a smile.

Adapt to the changed environment whether you like it or not. Change is inevitable.

Even wind chimes irritate a disturbed mind. Let your mind relax and start afresh.

If your intentions are honest then, you don't need to explain anything to anyone.

You may not grow rich if the focus is only on money. Grow rich in terms of blessings received in return for your kindness. Grow rich in terms of knowledge gained and multiplied through sharing and applying. Grow rich in terms of happiness experienced through your good deeds and innovation introduced.

The tough situation in life makes you strong. Be ready to face it.

Wish happiness for the world and Lord fulfills your wish.

We are generally quick in disliking certain things or people in our life. Instead of this it would be great if we can focus on our likes.

Share the gift of smile with the world.

Change yourself instead of trying the same with the other.

© **Look forward in your life**
BY SANDEEP RAVIDUTT SHARMA

It's a great day today. You are here to win.

Think big but never hesitate to do big.

Relax for a while and you will be alright.

Migrate from selfishness to selflessness stage in your life to improve your happiness quotient.

Not every time thing would turn out the way you want. In all kinds of situation God's wish prevails.

When you stick to responsible behaviour, don't bother about the world.

Face the world with grit and determination or the world will show you faces which you make not like.

Understanding is critical for conflict resolution.

Everyone wants to settle down in life but the final settlement nobody likes as it is to depart from this world.

© **Look forward in your life**
BY SANDEEP RAVIDUTT SHARMA

You don't have to run after happiness as it's within you.

Holding grudge against others is sure shot way of cultivating unhappiness. Forgive, and you become richer and happy every minute.

Take up the laughter challenge and you don't get affected by failure anymore.

Don't hesitate to raise your hand if you want to volunteer for a noble cause.

© **Look forward in your life**
BY SANDEEP RAVIDUTT SHARMA

Real friends are always there for you whether the times are good or bad.

Those who dare to accept their failure today ultimately become winner tomorrow.

The relationship is a two-way commitment.

Don't get attached to the shore if you intend to meet your destiny on the other side of the Ocean.

All your miseries can go to sleep only if you decide to be happy.

Take a snap of your happiness; it helps to motivate self during dark days.

Performance par excellence is achievable when passion and your heart is involved.

Don't get disappointed if your day did not turn up as per your thought. Tomorrow is another day.

Look forward and you can turn hope into Success soon.

www.ingramcontent.com/pod-product-compliance
Lightning Source LLC
Chambersburg PA
CBHW031440210526
45464CB00005B/2274